Bringing The Inside Out

Bringing The Inside Out

The words of people living in, working in,
and visiting care and nursing homes across
the UK during the Covid pandemic, 2020.

Living Words

Living Words
Living Words Arts
GF05, Glassworks
Mill Bay
Folkestone CT20 1JG
United Kingdom

First published in 2020
Text © 2020 Living Words

Illustrations & book cover © 2020 by Julia Miranda
juliamiranda@me.com

Bringing The Inside Out
www.livingwords.org.uk
info@livingwords.org.uk
+44(0)7967502506

ISBN 978-1-5272-8060-1

This anthology is dedicated to all those living with a dementia whose lives were lost due to the Covid-19 pandemic in 2020, to the carers who were with them, and their families, friends, and loved ones.

Contents

Forewords
    Brian Cox CBE, Actor   1
    Vic Rayner, Executive Director,   2
    National Care Forum (UK)
    Professor Sebastian Crutch,   3
    UCL Dementia Research Centre

Introduction
    Susanna Howard, charity founder,   5
    and Reinhard Guss, Living Words trustee

Bringing The Inside Out

THE KEY   11

Well, I feel   13
Helpless   14
The Most Difficult Thing   15
'Because, because'   16
Frustration   17
So Sad   18
The Key   19
Love is the only word really   20
Emotional to see her   21
Heart wrenching   22
'I am frustrated at the moment'   23
Here   24
Losing Nanna   25
Hold my hand   26
Change 2   27
Why me?   28
Frustrations and perseverance   29
Acceptance   30

I will remember that   31
Joy   32
'I feel okay today'   33
Pain of relationships   34
Another world   35
Deeply Sad   36
Unfair   37

Images   38

UNTETHERED   41

Floating Around   42
Segregation   43
11.   44
Lost   45
Sad times   46
Two observations   47
Lost time   48
Forgotten people   49
Loneliness   50
Just living   51
'I think, I feel and I see this double isolation'   52
Canadian Pacific   53
'Without you I'm wasted'   54
The need for human contact   55
Support   56
'Very good'   57

HE'S STILL THERE   59

'Shock'   61
12.   62
So much has changed   63

Losing touch   64
It's just a blur again   65
The hard times   66
Losing Friends   67
'It's like a bereavement but she's still here'   68
Guilt   69
It's best to talk about it   70
I'm grieving   71
'Awful'   72
'But of course, there's a great deal of guilt'   73

Images   74

PART OF THE PICTURES   77

Rooms   79
1.   80
4.   81
Family   82
It is how I feel   83
'Shutdown happened on the 23rd of March'   84
Making Light of a Bad Situation   85
We learned how to work in a team   86
Muffled Words   87
90   88
In through the nose, out through the mouth   89
TV   90
'You have to live in hope'   91
A smile wins it all   92
Part of the pictures   93
Digital – the answer?   94
Close Contact   95
6.   96

STAY ON THE SAME LINE   97

We Are Fighting You, Covid   99
'One of the carers I spoke to'   100
Solidarity   101
'If they can live through a war...'   102
Cariad Mawr, Un Amor Grande 2   *103*
My Personal Rollercoaster   104
Don't Forget   105

ARE WE NEARLY THERE YET?   107

She wouldn't be able to answer me now   109
The Abandonment   110
Sums it up   111
Don't like being critical   112
Written down   113
Who Cares?   114
Boredom Area   115
I don't want to blame   117
Who's got the power?   118
Forgotten   119
Are we nearly there yet?   120
'I don't know'   121
Slow motion   122
'Well, I don't know how it is'   123
We're human too   125

Images   126

THE FAMILY'S EYES   129

Family and support   131
Not just a Job   132

My thoughts again   133
Her wee face was so lit up   134
It's just the situation now   135
Emm   136
'I feel a bit, y'know, sad for the residents'   137
My Extended Family   138
Fear   139
'At this moment I'm feeling good'   140
My Mum   141
Children   142
So much love around you, if you open your eyes   143
My Mum and Dad   144
'I think that we are families for our residents'   145
'Sally, Sally, Pride of our alley'   146

ONLY HUMAN   147

Silver Lining   149
'We are only human'   150
'Hello'   151
Very Lucky   152
Ordinary Life   153
I Just Don't Know   154
The Sea   155
'Look at you'   156
Photos   157
'About life'   158
Cariad Mawr, Un Amor Grande   159
'Just fine'   160
The Middle   161

THE TOLL OF THE MASK   163

The Deceit   165

'Very tired'   166
Very true   167
It's quite sad actually   168
We have to look after each other   169
Go away Covid   170
The Toll of The Mask   171
Just Show Love   172
Touch   173
Put them down   174
'I don't think he'll live longer than...'   175
You lose some   176
Mental Health   177
The old me   178
Don't Know   179
BETTER   180
The All Singing, All Dancing Show   181
A better side   182
I care because I love to   183
'I just wanna be getting back'   184
Fine   185
When you get good care...   186
Motivation   187
'It is so, so difficult, you know'   188
Red Tape   189
Safety   190
Element of luck   191
We are working hard   192
Making A Difference   193
'We are in here'   194
You Do Get Fed Up With Things   195
'Do you know what I love doing?'   196
'We plod on because we love it'   197

Images   198

RAISE YOUR VOICES!   201

'Every resident we have here ...'   203
Voices   204
The Best Life   205
It's structural   206
The Four Nations   207
Raise your voices!!   208
Thanks to the carers   209
Sod the consequences   210

LIVING, LIVING   211

The Light at the End of the Tunnel   213
'Look at all that writing'   214
'You see. Happy'   215
Definitely   216
'I gotta gotta'   217
I Am Quite Happy   218
Angela's girl   219
'As I'm speaking to you now'   220
'To be loved'   221
7.   222
Living   223
Nature reflection   224

INDEX   225
THANKS   230
Feedback for 'Bringing the Inside Out', 2020   232
Leaving a Legacy Gift or Making a Donation   233

Forewords

It is a privilege for me to write the foreword for this book. I am deeply impressed by the work done in our care homes by teams of dedicated and inspiring health care professionals, having witnessed first-hand the support my beloved sister Bette has received in the Dalweem care home in Aberfeldy. The good work done for the well-being of our most vulnerable citizens can never be commended enough. These unprecedented times have created unforeseen challenges for so many and yet the fortitude of our care worker community, throughout this crisis, has provided a formidable example to us all. It is an honour for me to support their voices.

Brian Cox, CBE, 12th November 2020

The words of the people in *Bringing The Inside Out* will resonate with care home residents, their loved ones and professional carers, and with all of us as a society. This book is a living witnessing of words. I have followed the work of Living Words with huge admiration and great interest as an example of innovation, and am delighted to be writing this foreword.

In this book we can really hear not only the human cost of confusion but the incredible resilience and care given by those on the front line having to adapt to a rapidly changing world. This book is an outstanding arts project that provides a unique and invaluable insight into how things have really been through the pandemic. It reveals much that can't be easily measured through quantitative data.

It's been incredible to see the strong public backing for the sector continue to grow despite a strong media focus largely on bad news. So many professional carers and families have expressed feelings of being misrepresented or not heard in the coverage during this pandemic. It's so important to bring some balance to the story by showcasing some of the creative ways professional carers and activity coordinators have gone above and beyond to try to compensate for the lack of family interaction during the lockdown on visiting. The words in the book illustrate how front line professional carers have made huge sacrifices to provide the best quality care they can in this extraordinary time.

It is vital to listen if we want to really hear the words of those on the front line, and to have policy and guidance that works. We need to ensure we foster a culture of transparency where people are given the time and encouragement to share their experiences. This book is an invaluable guide to hearing the words of the people on the front line of this pandemic.

The words in this book highlight the importance of relationships, and the sense of community that is at the heart of great care.

We need to listen to these words, and we need to keep listening. Let's make 2021 the year of social care reform.

Vic Rayner, 30th November 2020
Executive Director, National Care Forum (NCF)

Of many stark realities over the past few months, the fact that people with dementia account for 25% of all COVID-19 related deaths in England and Wales is among the most sobering. With many of those terrible losses and bereavements seemingly linked to death rates in care homes, and with the eyes of the world often focused elsewhere, most of us will never be able to appreciate the desperate decisions and traumatic realities experienced by those living and working in the care home sector. Caught between lack of central guidance and varying local regulations, care homes and the staff and residents who are their lifeblood, have been stretched and strained as never before. All the while, family and friends on the outside have often had to share that painful separation, and witness the impact of loneliness and lost affection on those dearest to them.

This remarkable volume brings together the perspectives of residents, care staff, and relatives to offer unique insights into the lives of those buffeted at the centre of the storm. With dementias affecting not just memory but language, perception, decision-making and other skills we rely on to understand the world around us and our place within it, Living Words' creative, flexible and personal approaches to supporting people to find and share their voices are invaluable. Within these pages, the stories of those too often marginalised in our society are given space to breathe, and the true human cost of this pandemic may be found.

Sebastian Crutch, 26th November 2020
Professor of Neuropsychology
Dementia Research Centre, UCL
Co-lead, Rare Dementia Support
raredementiasupport.org

Introduction

Welcome to Living Words' 'Bringing The Inside Out'.

This book comprises the words of over 65 people who live in, work in, and visit care homes across the UK. They are the words of people who have survived the Covid 19 pandemic to the end of November 2020

These words represent the pieces that make up the personal books of each person who took part in the project. Every person's books are for them to keep and share with their friends and family, or to keep as something just for themselves.

The methodology that we use at Living Words is called Listen Out Loud. It is a way of shared listening and co-creation, in which the speaker speaks, the writer writes, and the way that the words land on the page represent how the person has said them, so that, in the reading back, the speaker hears themselves clearly, has ownership and validation. We have been working in this way since 2007.

This project came about following a light consultancy towards the end of England's first lockdown. Professional care staff told us that they felt isolated from the experiences that they knew other care staff across the country were facing. They felt unheard, and unseen – by each other, and the wider world. As we have been unable to run projects in care homes since the start of the pandemic, Living Words has needed to be agile.

Prior to the pandemic we had been looking to explore online learning to expand the reach of our work, and so we decided to bring this forward. 'Bringing The Inside Out' began with piloting remote action learning sessions with care staff across the UK. We were keen to not be defined by our locality in the South East of England, and to connect across all four nations. Week by week we trained care staff in our Listen out Loud methodology, as they each trialled the method with residents in their care and nursing homes. Across the 16 care homes, 34 people with a dementia received their words, some of which are featured in this book. An unexpected outcome of these sessions was the camaraderie, connection and warmth felt from East Kilbride to Torfaen, from County Antrim to The Wirral, from Norfolk to West Riding to Kent.

Our team of artists on this project were Anil Sebastian, Oliver Senton, Shazea Quraishi, Susanna Howard and Zoë Aldrich. Following the remote action learning, each of us worked one-to-one, on the telephone this time rather than in person, with all the carers from the action learning, plus more care staff from other homes across the country. We wrote their words down about their experiences of the pandemic. And we spoke with relatives, listening and writing down their words about how they were feeling, how they have been impacted and how their relationships with their loved ones have been challenged.

I would like to take a moment to honour all of the care homes who have taken part in this project. Those who have chosen to be named are featured in our 'Thanks' at the back of this book. The bravery of the speakers and the bravery of their managers and providers means a great deal to us, as I know it will to you.

It has been a tremendous and daunting task to whittle down the pieces from the thousands co-created, to under two hundred. We have been wracked with nerves and unsure of ourselves every step of the way. But this is the shape of the book right now. And we thank the understanding and continued support we have received from participants and readers alike. You will notice that there are pieces throughout that are attributed 'Anon'. Through doing this, voices can be heard that might otherwise have been fearful of going into print, for whatever reason. And finally, we have chosen not to tell you 'this is a person with a dementia' or 'this is a carer' or 'this is a relative' in the main body of the book. If you so choose, you can look this up in the Index.

In reading these pieces, you will only hear the voice of one person who lost their relative during the pandemic. This person is close to the organisation and we chose to include them. The voices of the many relatives who have lost members of their family to the pandemic is perhaps, another book. Our love and thoughts go to them, to you.

Our vision for 2021 is to create a bespoke Living Words touring van. A van we can live in, create a stage on, and run workshops from. We want to travel to each of the areas in the UK represented in this project and bring 'Listen Out Loud' trainings, book readings, performances and song to the people living in, working in, and visiting care homes, and the wider communities in these areas. That's the dream.

We believe that if we truly listen, we give another the validation and belief to express themselves, free from shame, wholly as we are. We believe that if this happens, there is no need for binary conversations that point towards blame. Through truly hearing another's experience, we can build towards a better future. This is our aim.

Susanna Howard, 30th November 2020
Living Words founder, and artistic director

Listen Out Loud, the Living Words methodology used in care homes with people with late stages of dementia, has resulted in extraordinary insights into the experience of people often seen as beyond meaningful communication. The beauty, clarity, and poetry of these words, faithfully recorded, has long accompanied me in my professional life as a Clinical and Neuropsychologist with a passion for refining the uses of psychological therapies for people living with dementia.

The changed world of the COVID pandemic has had a particularly devastating impact in care homes, and especially on people with dementia, their relative, and those working closely with them day by day as carers. It has also stopped the work of Living Words within care homes, and made it impossible to use 'Listen Out Loud' in its usual form through trained and experienced artists. It has been an amazing feat of creativity to change the approach to something that could be used under these circumstances, and it is testament to the dedication of all involved that here again, we can experience insight, beauty, clarity, and poetry in the words of those most affected.

From my experience as a psychotherapist, I know about the power of being actively listened to, and from the experience of art, we know of the power of self-expression, both coming together in the pieces chosen from the books of 65 individual people, each with their own perspective. I hope that readers will be able to 'Listen Out Loud', even if just a little, while engaging with these texts, and gain some beauty, clarity and insight while engaging with these texts of some unique people, despite the difficulty of the times and experiences they describe.

Reinhard Guss, 30th November 2020
Living Words Trustee
Consultant Clinical Psychologist
Clinical Neuropsychologist

'The key'

Well, I feel

It continues
Yeah
I haven't
I get tired quick
I feel lonely
Sometimes

"Hellos" when
People come over
But they're not
Inside
They're outside

When you sort out
What you want
I go for that

I feel
it's hard

Wouldn't be if I could
Do more, see more
But
All that
Stopped.

Anon

Helpless

Some of it is silly things, really –
in the visitor room for instance, you know, if you
think...
she needs a tissue or something,
you know, she's not quite comfortable or something,
and it's fairly, um,
well normally, it'd be very easy
just to use a tissue to wipe her mouth,
or do, do those sort of minor things.
Or adjust her a little bit to make her a bit more
comfortable.
If a pillow, or a blanket or whatever is
slipping, or something.
When you're separated with a glass screen
you can't do that,
you just have to sort of watch.

Peter Jones

14

The Most Difficult Thing

I've seen her
but I haven't physically touched her since
the 16th of March.
Which is hard.

Because I always did her hair for her and
everything else.
So, I'm going to get my hands on her hair
and sort that out.

For six months, I was sleeping in the same
bed with her, looking after her, after we lost
Dad.
That's hard.
Especially when she puts her hand up
to the glass and wants...
she wants a hug.

She doesn't understand you can't do that.

Ceri Clarke

Because, because
normally she is in the big sitting room
when we go round to the window
because she doesn't know me, it just...
she's taken to her bedroom to sit, to speak to us
she'll sit at the window in a chair, a small window open
and she can barely hear us, let alone anything else
she just, she just...
if there's somebody there, there's a conversation
you know, between me and them and trying to include
her
but she doesn't know
her answer will be...
well, she doesn't really answer
there's no conversation anymore
but there was conversation
six months ago
not a lot, don't get me wrong
we could talk about the old days

Roxella

Frustration

Now they've had in-house visits start
I had one the other week
I fully understand the rigmarole you have to go through
–

But I turn up,
And my Dad wasn't even out of bed
I was really miffed
I'd taken time out of work
I had to organize that, had to ask special permission

And I just find that every time there's an email,
It's all changed
You get yourself into the way of thinking:
"Oh good, I'll be seeing Dad such and such, or whatever"
And then the plan changes
That's the most frustrating thing
It's not just straightforward, anything

I can imagine it's upsetting all-round for the staff as
well,
But they're really a great team of people
Nothing's too much trouble
I imagine it must be quite a strain for them
'Cause they've had to go to work
and their families are at home

You just don't know what's the situation,
And what's going to happen

Anon

17

So Sad

With the pandemic
I've only seen him about six times
for an hour at a time
through a window. With a mask on,
and he's deaf and he can't lip-read.
Just heart breaking.
He doesn't know who I am now because he hasn't seen
me.

I just don't know what to do.
I've got to keep going
but it's so pointless. Heart breaking.
I honestly think he thinks that we've all forgotten him.
Which doesn't help him
and it doesn't help me but
I have to go.

Mavis Eyre

The Key

Horrible
They can't
I can't join in
With them

See them
Be part of it
But I can't

Have calls
And windows
But it's not the same
What they call it?
The key

Key
Just the key
An ordinary key
To keep me together
I feel as though
I'm doing something

Anon

Love is the only word, really

I've got three quarters of an hour drive to see her
Only on the outside
Through a tight window
that can only open three inches
Can't be opened wide
They're on a lock

She has Parkinson's
She's very quiet talking
I can't hear her very well especially if it's windy
I want to get closer to the windows
So I put the mask on
Although she's used to the mask from the home
it's not great because she can't see my mouth
That affects me more than anything

Jane

20

Emotional to see her

It's been really hard.
My Dad hasn't seen her, because he's more or
less house bound, me Dad,
We look after him.
He's dead strong – mind and everything.
Very stubborn. And strong.
A couple of times he has been to see her, she's
not really made any contact with him.
That's really, really hurt him. So
he hasn't been. Well, with the
lockdown, none of us have
been.

Dad found it really, really hard,
her not acknowledging him.
I report to him everyday how she is.
And as long as she's fine,
and healthy,
and she seems happy,
it seems to help him.

Barbara Osborne

21

Heart wrenching

Seeing her at a window -
It's just horrible
And my mother has Alzheimer's
she doesn't really understand what's going on
Sometimes she would sit and cry
She felt that she was being punished
Because she wasn't allowed out

I couldn't comfort her
She doesn't understand
It breaks my heart
As if someone put their hand in my chest
And pulled my heart out
It's heart wrenching

It's how she puts her hand to the window
Sometimes I have to sit and laugh with her
I can't say how I really feel to her

Susan McCallum

I am frustrated at the moment
Hmm things,
Things in my private life

I can't see my wife or daughter

Elliot

Here

A lot of our residents haven't had any contact
with their family –

They haven't come to the windows
They haven't video-called
They haven't telephone-called

They just haven't come

Anon

Losing Nanna

It's been tough on them
It's tough on my family too
Because her grandkids can't just go
They would have to book an appointment
Or they try and come with me
But when they're working, they can't

One of my children really struggles
He just really gets upset when he goes in
He said, "It's just so sad,
It's not fair we can't go when we want to go"
I think he's going to come with me today because he's
off
But you can see him getting all anxious about it
If he can't hold her hand
He does just tear up and walk outs
It affects everybody

Lynne Ellis

Hold my hand

But it's the contact
I miss that contact and she does too
She puts her hand up for me to take her hand and I can't
She wants a hug -
I want to hug but I can't -
So the staff have to hug her
I'm sitting there thinking 'That's my job'
You know? It is very very hard
I've struggled a lot with it

Lynne Ellis

Change 2

Home did become home to them
- their lounge or wherever they were.
Then we changed the rules
That brought its own challenges:
residents were seeing their family
for 20 minutes, half an hour -
they wanted longer.

They were coming back sad, depressed,
annoyed they couldn't hug their family member.
You thought, as much as they miss their family,
are we doing the right thing?

                                        Jennifer Carson

Why me?

Then they had these garden visits
There's been lots of chops and changes recently
We had Skype calls as well as the garden visits
Different days were for different parts of the building
I only managed to get one in, one visit,
Because somebody tested positive
And then they had to cancel them
So those sorts of inconveniences, not due to anyone's
fault, came along,
And it was difficult
I had another one booked, and they rang me:
"Oh, would you mind if we give that to somebody else,
because they haven't managed to get one? "
Well, they caught me on the hop
What could I say? I said
"Oh yes, fine. No problem"
Cause I had one later, the following week or something
And then they cancelled them
Because somebody tested positive
That was what happened on and off
If someone tests positive, they have to cancel all the
visits

I fully understand that I'm being very selfish,
But it affected me, you know
So that was that

Anon

28

Frustrations and perseverance

My Mum has a gripper, we call it a gripper,
a handle with a claw -
so, we open the window and we can chat
if it's wet, I sit in the car, she can see me
and I can 'phone her,
so we have a visual on each other -
but if I'm handing sweeties through the window
and the claw, she loses grip
I can see her trying to pick up the sweets
and you know, she's really determined
but it would take me seconds, to run round
pick them up and give them to her
but she has to persevere
and I find it frustrating, standing at the window

Mrs Avril Hamilton

Acceptance

When he went into the home
I couldn't go and see him
We chose a small one not too far away
We couldn't see what room he had or anything else
because of the limitations of COVID

When he was settled we went to see him
We could only see him in the garden
during the nice weather
We had to wear masks to see him
He'd got to the stage where he didn't really know us
His face would light up
You could see he was working out who we were

I would like to be there almost every day -
Seeing how he is, what the staff were like
Making sure that he was being looked after properly
and wasn't being neglected or anything

All these things go through your mind
Was he calling me and I wasn't there?

Barbara

I will remember that

She's trying to get me through the glass
She banged her head trying to kiss me
And she says,
"Oh, blackened me nose! Blackened nose!"
and she rubbed her nose
I said, "Oh Mum!"
And she grinned at me
She was trying to kiss me
Oh she's a little sweetie

Lynne Ellis

Joy

She's happy there
I went there to go to her birthday
I could see her opening her presents
It's so difficult to see through double glazing
You get your own reflection
You know, little things like that

I did take a cracker
Had been in the house since last year
I put gel before I got the cracker out
Made sure it was all sprayed
I took it through to her

I poked it through the window
We pulled the cracker together
The joy of being able to pull something together
was lovely
It's like holding each other

Jane

I feel okay today
like doing things - reading

I can do better or more things,
I like to

I can do a little, always happy to
come here

Listening to the radio, enjoying the
sun, meeting people, yes I do

I like going out to meet people

Anon

Pain of relationships

The families -
I think they feel as much as the residents about not
seeing each other -

And I'm not too sure whether
It kind of polarises people's emotions
Some families will try every day to make an effort
while others feel 'Well, we can't do anything'
So that's it - will lead to
'Well, we only can see her once a month' instead of once
a week

Generalising
But habits change

Marian Howell

Another world

Since March we've seen her three four times
We're allowed to make an appointment this week

If they haven't seen you
That's when they start forgetting
Who you actually are
Which will be the hardest thing to accept

Jackie Law

Deeply Sad

Eventually on the 9th of September - Mum and Dad's
Platinum Wedding Anniversary, 70 years -
I managed to get an appointment to go and see them
And when it was finished, I was wishing I hadn't

They were brought out to a canvas gazebo
- wind was blowing a gale, it was cold -
Dad had no socks on
his trousers halfway up his leg
didn't know who I was
He asked the carer "Who is this?"

Mum recognised me
even though I was wearing a mask -
I looked straight at her
and stared for a few seconds, said "Hello Mum"
and she lifted her hand, and she was smiling
She used to always do that if a visitor was coming

Anon

Unfair

I just wish I could hold her hand through the glass
I wish there was a little cubby hole we could make
She doesn't understand
why I can't open the door and talk to her

She'd try and tell me and pull on the door
And I'd say, "I can't Mum it's broken"
And she lifted her eyes to the sky as if to say *Huh!*
Goodness me she was *not* very happy
It's hard on her
She doesn't understand why
Her Lynne would always hold her hand

Lynne Ellis

Anil Sebastian

Suzanne Elliot

Kathleen Crymble

Leanne

Lainey and Jenny

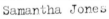

Samantha Jones

Chloe
Crawford

Ian McOnie

'Untethered'

Floating Around

Bloody Awful
I would like to go home
And sit forever
But I don't know where home is

They all ran away
Or maybe I ran away

I don't know

I've lost my memory completely

I'm just feeling how
Wondering what's going to happen
Just floating around

I'm just here
Just floating around

Round the bend
Or only half way

I'm fully round the bend
Probably
Twice round

Anon

Segregation

It's a very difficult thing,
unless you've experienced it
unless you really care for somebody who's in that
environment
I don't think that people realise the devastating effects

I've seen some close friends lose family members from
care homes
how they've had to deal with that loss
not being able to see that family, not being able to...
hold their hand and be with them, when they pass away
because they couldn't.
And deal with the funeral afterwards and all of those
things.

But what about the ones that are still alive?
That are still yearning to see their family?
I want people to think about that.

Jacqui Offen

II.

You also got to know the relatives of the other people,
you'd have little chats
little group of you
me and my wife talking to somebody and their daughter
or their husband, you know
you feel part of a little community.

All those encounters have –
have stopped.

I've not seen any of the other residents.
Since March.

Peter Jones

Lost

Lost
I think there are so many people who are lost in all of
this
You know, not knowing, not understanding or
appreciating what's going on

I think there will be a huge proportion of people who
feel lost
Untethered

Mrs Avril Hamilton

Sad times

I'm convinced it's affected my Mum

Her family are now staff in the home
That's who she looks to for a cuddle
We've lost that connection

Even the other residents who I saw
In March they were really quite with it still
I saw one the other day as their visitors were leaving
You get such a shock
It's as though he looked at me as if to say, "I know you"
and so I waved to him and he was like, "Oh-oh right hi
hi"

It's for them as well
The other residents
Not seeing other people coming in
It must feel awful
Like prison
It really must

Lynne Ellis

Two observations

One where you feel well
One you feel useful

Someone takes it away
And you end up with nothing

Or end up
Doing something then
Something
Makes it difficult
To do anything

Mess up
My thoughts
Mess up

New machine
A new something to help
It might work

But I haven't got a job
I want to
But I can't

Confused

Anon

Lost time

But I think the nature of the illness in here
the residents not really remembering
it sometimes makes it even harder.
They don't remember that they've not seen anybody
and that's, that's quite heartbreaking

Also for the visitors -
heartbreaking for the relatives who can't get in.
There was a man used to come in every day
spend most of the day
would help feed his wife, lunch time and dinner time.
And that man has not been allowed to come in since
March.

Heartbreaking for him and for his wife as well
it's not easy at all.

Suzanne Elliot

Forgotten people

If I didn't have my mother in a care facility I probably
wouldn't think about how a person's life has changed

People in residential care facilities are a forgotten
society
That's what I feel
And that breaks my heart
Opens up a can of worms
Makes me think of their life value
If it wasn't for these people
we wouldn't have what we have today
We need to fight for other people's rights

They're locked in there
They've been forgotten
It's times like this we need to start looking outside
There's other people outside your own bubble

Susan McCallum

Loneliness

It's been stressful because I'm not a bad asthmatic, but I
do have asthma.
I had a positive COVID in May this year.
I was on me own, obviously isolated.
It was good, I didn't have to worry about anyone else at
work. But then I found it lonely.

Mum came round to drop some food off.
As she was walking away from my front door, I'm
staying well back, but I knew she'd come specially,
Almost hurt more, if that makes sense?
I was thinking, that's horrible, and I can't tell her that,
she'd be even more upset.

Ian McOnie

Just living

Many people don't realise -
Because of the industry we work in
nothing stopped for us
We are essential workers
We have to keep going

We haven't done anything
we're not able to travel
we're not able to go anywhere

If you have days off
You can't go out -
You can't do anything
So you just feel it is better to just be at work instead

Kunle Olaifa

I think, I feel and I see this double isolation
not just in my own home
also, in the workplace.
Because families can't visit our residents,
all the support and energy is from us.

But I really love what I do.

For this type of work, you need to have the heart,
the soul.

Margarita Warburton

Canadian Pacific

As long as I go
But I can't work out a lot of things

I used to know

But I can't work it out

How things came to me
Things going one
But is there

I made it back to my home
And my true love

I don't know what that is
People move along you see

Yeah
People move along

Anon

Without you I'm wasted

alright

You didn't like that

I feel alright otherwise I would have gone

Anon

The need for human contact

I feel as if there are lost souls in there
All these residents
They're doing activities and all the rest of it
But that's not hugs
That's not holding hands
Like a lot of people, I'm a huggy person

Irene McGinney

Support

I said to one of the nurses,
With everything going on,
you can't get the support in your life from your friends
and family.
You can't go around for a cup of tea and have a chat
and talk about what was on TV or whatever.

Little things like that.
Just to chat to someone about football or music
or daft stuff like what's on the telly, or what you've
been doing the day before.
That sort of thing helps you, doesn't it?

Ian McOnie

Very good
Tomorrow, I don't like

Anon

'he's still there'

Shock
Horrendous.
Absolutely horrendous.

At the beginning of it I think I had seen my parents -
in February, early March
Was busy thinking, it'll be okay in a few weeks
and a few weeks, became months and
I mean, I was pining for them,
particularly my Mum.

And that's got dramatically worse over the months -
situations like, 'Oh, I'd love to tell my Mum that'
or, 'I would love to phone her' -
but because she's got dementia, she doesn't do
telephones anymore

And the stress was building up and building up –
on the 20th of June, I looked in the mirror
and the whole of the right side of my face had fallen

Called paramedics and at first
they thought it was a stroke, but it was Bell's Palsy
I discussed it with the paramedic
he had several cases in the same week
And he was sure that stress causes a lot of Bell's Palsy

So that was me - I was housebound
I wouldn't go out with my face like that, down there
Housebound for about a month
My husband did everything for me.

Irene McGinney

12.

At the start, people weren't allowed
to go into the homes to see their elderly relative passing
away
they weren't able to sit there by their side
weren't able to
share them last few months with them
and I think for the actual residents
been awful for them and I think
yeah, it's really important that people know and
that people
understand how hard that is
and to see, as a carer

and to kind of be there for them as their families -
well, obviously,
you try and be there for someone, but you're not their
daughter or
you're not their relative

I think, yeah,
it's important that people know that, and people
understand that this is
real

Megan Whitworth

62

So much has changed

I feel like I'm completely split
and have been for quite a while
Feel like so much I'm accepting and that's fine
And I'm coping and getting on with it

Not much of life for us at home has really changed that
much because at least I have worked all the way
through it. But then on the other hand so much has
changed.

So the whole of the last six months
I've been sort of two people

Had to be very normal and get on with things
Go to work and cope and take responsibility
Help people to cope with losing people
that they haven't been able to see
Family members who have been with them for 80 years
all this history and still lots and lots of life to live
And it just hasn't been
their time
I just feel
it's not been their time

Anon

Losing Touch

It's so so hard
when you've lived with a person so long.
Now I'm thinking, my David's dead.
He's not my David, he's a complete stranger.
So hard.

But nobody's got an answer, have they?
We can't do anything.
Until all this horrible pandemic's gone.
But it's too late for people with dementia then.
They're losing touch with the people that love and care
for them.

Mavis Eyre

64

It's just a blur again

I'm only 21
Seeing so many deaths in such a short period of time is
obviously going to have an effect
I knew it was going to happen
It's so hard to see

It's emotional isn't it?
I'm quite emotional
I've been working
you've got to get on with it
Just try and blank it out
Try and move forward
Carry on

I keep myself busy
That's what keeps me going
Work keeps me going at the minute

I just want it to be over
Next year
A New Year

Chloe

The hard times

We've had to deal with dying residents -
That's not nice, especially when you've grown a bond
with them throughout the years

Honestly, dealing with the COVID patients has got to be
the most challenging bit -
The most hardest
I struggled with that the most

The deaths

Chloe Crawford

Losing Friends

They have lost a few people through COVID –
I think, well I know several people who died over the
summer.
People who, you thought,
Oh, you know, they're mobile, they're walking around,
they're perhaps, you know, feeding themselves,
they're - seem to be in quite a good position.
But sadly, they... died.
Over the summer.
And that's a bit of a shock.

Peter Jones

It's like a bereavement but she's still here.
I'm grieving for my Mother. But she's still here.
I am still grieving for her.

Roxella

Guilt

It's true
It's what I feel
I'm just lost for words
I feel like a blank

And then there's the guilt

Terrible guilt
because I think
If I'd went up every day -
would she still recognise me?

Roxella

It's best to talk about it

He was used to have lots of tools
He had boats, engines, motorbikes
He was like Steptoe
Collected all these bits and pieces
I've got to sell all these things
The money will go towards the fees
I'm financing myself
Costing me an arm and a leg
And I feel guilty about selling all these bits and pieces
I know they've got to go
I can't hang on to all these things

Every week I seem to dream about him
And it's always as he was
I can have a word with him and goodness knows what
And I'm thinking to myself in the dream
As I'm talking to this person that he was
I've got to be careful I don't want him to know
I've sold all his bits and pieces because he'll get upset
So, I've got that deep down guilt that I'm selling his
things but he's still there

Barbara

I'm grieving

A lot of people don't understand
It's been eight months of this and it's horrendous
That's eight months
I've missed my proper normal contact with her

In a funny way you do feel like you're grieving
I know they say it's the long goodbye Alzheimers
But it's just made it a hundred times worse
I do feel as though I'm grieving
I really do

I keep thinking
She's still here though
but she's not
She's here in person -
but I can't be close with her

Lynne Ellis

Awful

No I'm just joking

About life?

Well
How I'm feeling
Oh God
Don't go and leave me

I can't open it

That ain't bad weather
Really is it

But of course
They're all locked up
Over there
All locked up
Yeah

Well, I feel
Alright
I suppose
Yeah

Anon

But of course, there's a great deal of guilt.
That I'm not with my wife.

I spent twelve years looking after my wife.
As the disease progressed.
It was getting quite difficult.
Which is why she moved into the home.
So, I mean I also feel guilt because I can't really help her.

Peter Jones

Mrs Warrior113

Margarita Warburton

Peter Jones

Abi Watt

Janice Dye

Hollis Jones

Susanna Howard

Lynne Ellis

Irene McGinney

Naomi Daglish

'Part of the pictures'

Rooms

At one point, we had to have all of the residents in
their rooms, at the beginning of lockdown,
Which obviously, with people with dementia,
It was tough
It was hell for everybody really
The residents didn't understand
And I think in a way, it just -
Everything just stopped

It used to be such a live, bustling home
We would have a quiz and word games in the morning,
maybe finish off with a little bit of sing-along, then
we'd all go down to lunch together,
In the afternoon we would have a dance-to-music
exercise class, some kind of group activity, even if it was
just knocking a balloon around
So there was always something going on,
And the residents had a choice whether to be in their
room, or in the lounge, or in the corridor, or wherever
they wanted to be
And then it was just - Nope!
Got to be in your room
It was like a ghost town in here

Naomi Daglish

1

we were just kind of trying to...
do what we could to separate the residents
and help them out and try and keep them safe,
group them into bubbles,
did kind of off our own back,
in the first instance anyway.

So it was a bit uncertain
didn't really know what was going on.
And then obviously,
things got known a little bit more

And then, unfortunately,
the home got hit with the virus
and there were symptoms that we had no idea of,
that I suppose the government didn't really even know
of at the
time.

And then, unfortunately we got hit with it quite hard.
And we lost quite a few of our residents at the home
and yeah, life completely changed.

Megan Whitworth

4

I moved into the care home along with a couple of other
staff members,
and
lived there, just to help out

My family at home, my parents, they were classed as
vulnerable

Didn't want to leave the home without any help. So...
I moved into one of the rooms and lived there for
two and a half months, which was -

very worried times and very unexpected
and
yeah, just absolutely crazy.

Megan Whitworth

Family

I got accused of making it all up and I was like,
I'm not making it up

In this home, we've seen a few people pass away

I've been here for like 15 years and you get used to
seeing someone.

And when they're not there, it feels like - empty space
and you wonder
how the families are doing, because I
haven't seen any of the families,
so, I just want to know if they're okay,
but –
like I said, you take a day at a time

Seth Munday

It is how I feel

It's difficult to try and...
to say how we feel
without sounding bitter

I don't want to 'phone them every five minutes
to see how my Mother is
'cause I know they are busy
but I quite miss that, you know - asking
"How is she today? Has she been alright" or
"How was the sore that she's got on her forehead?"

I miss -
painting her nails, things like that
she'll be squealing when I cut them
but loves it when they are done

Feel extremely sad, sad I can't see her
and then mad, mad
a whole load of emotions that run with it

Roxella

Shutdown happened on the 23rd of March,
which happened to be my birthday -
I shall forever be remembered for that!
But this isn't about me –

They actually shut down two weeks before the official
lockdown happened
So, I was regularly still going to where my Dad lives, but
then handing in his grocery money and what he calls his
medicine (that's his flask of rum and coconut water)
through the window in the office to the staff
So, I was still doing the regular visits to my Dad's place,
but I couldn't go in

So, I'd literally be there in a carpark straddled on my
pushbike
Handing over a flask through the window of the office,
Plus, the odd box of Celebrations,
chocolates to say thank you to the care staff
And every time I drop off his rum
I quickly cycle round to the other side of the premises
Where I could look over through the railings,
and I'd say "Dad, just try and stand up, turn around,
and you can wave at me through the window"
which he did, and he had his phone to his ear. I say,
"Have you got your medicine? Give us the thumbs up"
He'd give me the thumbs up
and I know he'd be okay

So, I've been very grateful to staff
I felt peace of mind
knowing he's somewhere safe and secure

Samantha Jones

Making Light of a Bad Situation

We've looked at each other, the carers,
we've smiled at each other and your eyes do move.
So that the residents know we're smiling, we're not
making faces at them.

A couple of times I've joked with them, saying,
'under this mask, me tongue is out at you!'
That makes 'em laugh.
So that's a good thing.

We thought about doing pictures on us masks, but
didn't know if it compromised the integrity of the mask
We were going to put a smiley face on
but we tried one and it looked frightenin'
so we didn't bother.

We are trying all sorts.
Some of the residents have got teddies,
we've put face masks on, and have jokes with them.
So we're trying different things.

It's the same for everybody really.
It's just we're in direct contact with them.
I don't think people realise that, how could they.

Karen Potter

We learned how to work in a team

In the sense with the lockdown, things haven't changed
it's just got more to do
Literally more
in every single sense - time commitment.
We have done six, seven days a week, with half a day off
to ensure that there's not other people coming into the
home to put our people at risk and put ourselves at risk.

And throughout all this journey
we have been having each other's back
supporting each other, which made our team even
stronger. So much stronger.

It is a different world we live in now
And we have to do as much as we can on our path
every single person has done it here
Yeah, it's a good team, a good place to work at

Mrs Warrior113

Muffled Words

With my work,
Wearing full face mask -
It's difficult for the residents to understand
Trying to do a little bit of a singsong,
And they can't see my lips.
So that, I've adjusted to,
But I don't think I'll ever get used to it.

It's surprising how well the residents here have
adapted,
They've been really good,
But I find the most difficult part is the communication -
Somebody might be agitated and upset,
You're trying to support them, have a conversation,
And they're not seeing your full emotions,
They're not hearing you clearly.

I'm finding little ways of getting round it.
I've got pictures with words on them
And they might be able to understand them,
Simple - like sad with a sad face on there,
or happy -
But it's not the same is it?

Janice Dye

90

90, who takes that?

Not the way it stays in

It's good for you you know
It's done me some good

Anon

In through the nose, out through the mouth

I
My Mum is still a big part of my life
There's days I could just sit and cry
But if you were to ask me why
I couldn't put my finger on it
I think sometimes things get too much
And you look at everything in the one big pot
You know, everything's in the pot

It's when you hear of the deaths or
There's no visiting in the care homes or
Someone's been tested positive
You can put all that in to the big pot
and think 'What happens now?'

That means I don't get to see my Mum
Won't have that contact, even if it is just at a window
And you just put them all together

II

You need a wee stiff upper lip
We trip over a stone in the path
and then that's you - off
We all have a wee chip in our cup some days

At a time like this
I could have run away -
To a Caribbean Island

Susan McCallum

TV

Fine
Nothing
Just want to watch tv
Nothing
Alright
Leave that alone it's mine

Anon

You have to live in hope
Because the alternative is not good

Mrs Avril Hamilton

A smile wins it all

One thing for sure is that I'm still positive
I still have a smile
a different type of smile,
it's hidden in there -
not as bubbly as I used to be
But yeah, I'm still positive.
That's one thing for sure.

Not as bubbly
which I did notice
other people noticed as well.
My personality in that respect
my self-expression has changed
but I am still positive minded.
Thank God.

Mrs Warrior113

Part of the pictures

I feel
Feel part of things
What others do

All in one order
Look inside yourself
Try and do it without
Not taking an expense

Work on it
Just not used to
Gotta work on it
Explain

Anon

Digital - the answer?

Yesterday I did a Zoom concert
The sound wasn't so good
They don't relate to somebody on screen in the same
way
So digital can help a huge amount
but it doesn't always get that personal LIVE feeling
it's sometimes hard to replicate

I have people who are not on frontline
"Get more laptops"
But I have to be there
Literally sit there and do it for them
People not in touch don't realise
It's not always the answer

Marian Howell

Close Contact

It was completely -
Work's completely different
We had to cancel all the activities
We couldn't have no one coming in
Which the people weren't too happy about
We had to do that to protect our customers

So what we were doing
Instead of doing activities
We were one-to-one
Going round to the most vulnerable customers
Making sure they were okay
Having a chat with them
Stuff like that
Taking the loneliness away a bit
And I found that quite beneficial for my job role -
I got to know the customers a little bit more
Cause I had that time one-to-one with them, rather than
a group session
They got to know me, and I got to know them,
A little more better

So I have found the Covid experience quite beneficial,
in a strange way
I learnt a hell of a lot

Kay

6.

The symptoms that got brought out
weren't the symptoms that were experienced within
the elderly,
but obviously, nobody really knew what was going on
and what the symptoms were, but
things like sickness and diarrhoea,
things like that were never spoken about, but
they were the kind of things that were experienced
at the beginning of the virus - and so it's
quite challenging trying to manage and -
understand what we were going to be faced with
and then each kind of
experience of Corona was different for absolutely
everyone

And, it didn't
affect the person the same,
so that was really challenging to deal with.

I suppose just the masses of death that you kind of
experience
it was just kind of unheard of and kind of unexpected

Megan Whitworth

'stay on the same line'

We Are Fighting You, Covid

I've gone round with stickers today.
It's got a rainbow on it and it says
Going to be OK
So, the units I can't get through, I pushed them
underneath and said "Put them up!"
We're going to be OK, because that's what we do, we
fight, and we're gonna fight it.
I'm not a fighter
but I am.

Karen Potter

One of the carers I spoke to
she phoned me for some reason
(Dad had fallen again)
said she felt as if she was part of the war
and she was heading over the top.
That's it -
they're all fighting their own war

Irene McGinney

Solidarity

I think we all have to stay on the same line,
and do the battle together.
That's the most important thing I would like to come
across.
We are not alone,
we are all together against this virus,
and together we are strong.

If we act all together, in the same direction –
we might have had different glasses on each other,
but if we look in the same direction,
there is a good change to
win the battle, yes.

Kitty van Geel

If they can live through a war, we can cope with this

Understand that it's tough for the carers
The way that we're doing things at the moment
Don't know what we're doing any more than the public

We're just going on
Learning as we go on
It's all new isn't it?
It's new - it's scary - it's different

At the end of the day the majority of the people we look
after have been through a war
They're hardy as anything

If they can go through that,
we can go through this

Abi Watt

Cariad Mawr, Un Amor Grande 2

The pandemic has coincided with other situations in the
world,
like racism, immigration.
Someone like me,
seeing in the news, that there are people
who don't accept or want people who come from other
countries…

I would like, for these people to see
that we are giving care and love in these places of need,
being their hands,
their heart.
We are the words of life and of love for them.
If you love this land, you love the people of this land.

Margarita Warburton

My Personal Rollercoaster

I do allow myself to make mistakes,
I do allow myself to have a bad day, and –
at the end of the day, you go to bed, and…
the greatest thing I have, I have my own home,
I have my wages,
and not in danger or whatever.

So, I'm alright, I'm alright, yes.
Everybody has his own life
and you never know when you get up in the morning,
how do I go to bed tonight?
What happens, we don't know.
We have to accept these certain times,
times from bombing, to war, to fake news –
we all have to make our own way,
and find our own peace with it.

Kitty van Geel

Don't Forget

We will get through this.
Maybe not everybody will get through it.
But as a country, as a world,
there will be people here to carry it on, to talk about
this time.
This time will not be forgotten.
That's the important thing.
Let's not forget the people who didn't make it.
Also say thank you to people that have helped
the people with the Covid.

So hard to watch people die
and not be able to save them.
You can't save everybody.

Lainey

'Are we nearly there yet?'

She wouldn't be able to answer me now

I sometimes get angry because people go on about
dementia
but until you have lived with it, you cannot have a full
grasp

I find them so patronising, saying "It must be hard"
they have no idea how bad it is

and when we made the decision to put Mum in a
nursing home - they have no idea what we went
through before that

oddly, carers at the time, knew how bad things were
we battled all the way through

and to be knocked down by a virus
seems really cruel

we've battled for about ten years with dementia
at various stages, you know

and we kept it so she was happy
and she probably is happy at the nursing home

but I don't know!
because I never get the chance to ask her properly

without somebody, you know, being there as such,
and prompting her

Roxella

The Abandonment

I find that I'm quite disappointed
in a lot of ways -
things like doctors not coming into care homes.

At the beginning I saw letters sent to care homes from a
doctors' surgery
basically said 'You're on your own'
and I was pretty disgusted actually
when I saw it
thought it was disgraceful

And there was a lot of things happened I was quite
shocked by -
the DNRs having to get signed
end of life meds getting sent into care homes

At the very beginning it was quite scary
to the point of
you didn't know
how many people you were going to lose -
the way it was going you thought you might lose them
all
but that wasn't the way it ended up being

But it was quite, quite
scary at the beginning
we'd been more or less abandoned
- ambulances refused to come -
it was terrible
really terrible.

Kathleen Crymble

Sums it up

Not the most exciting
Boring and painful
That just sums it up
That's about it .... yes
Nothing is happening
It feels empty
Life there nothing happens

Mary Obgoboh

Don't like being critical

I don't know what else I can do
At the end of the day, it's a business
Bit ironic, isn't it, seeing as it's supposed to be the
caring profession
Who is it that they are caring for?

They still want to be able to say, after the pandemic
that they're still the same outstanding care home
that they were before.

And that's not necessarily what's behind closed doors.
Never know what's going on behind closed doors, do
you?

They are just so lucky that they've got
the people that they've got
working there, that have stayed and,
you know, sacrificed
done what they've been asked of 100 times over...

And more

Anon

Written down

It's been good
In the past
When the
Monday
Wednesday
Of each week
I don't
Improve things

Record
Next
Invoices

The second part
Like the second part
Feel let down
Haven't got anything

Makes me feel
Old
And hopeless

Whatever I do
  Is wrong
It shouldn't be
  But it is

That's right

Anon

Who Cares?

I've heard people say 'Well, it's only the old people.'
'Well, it's only the people in the care homes',
and I'd like to say to those people,
'What if that was your Mum, or your Dad, or your
brother or
your sister?
That you were talking about?'

And –
many of them, didn't know that my Dad was in a care
home.
that he's in palliative care, in late-stage dementia,
they don't know those things
and yet they would say those words.
I think they haven't really put themselves in someone's
shoes...

Maybe some people don't care about their elderly
family members,
have no
emotional intelligence to put themselves there.

But, I'd like them to know what it's like
so that perhaps they would think about it a little bit,
and consider,
just consider other people's feelings.

Jacqui Offen

Boredom Area

There's nothing to talk about
Not really

No

There's lots of things
All boredom
Boredom here
Boredom

Nothing fun
No

I say
Waste of time

Nothing more
No
My own life
As I go
Yeah

I know too much
In a way

Want to be settled
Settled

No good here
Around about here
Across the way
Boredom area

Area

Boredom area
No one else speak to me
No one else

Boredom area

I don't know
Stuck
Stuck here
Don't want it

Anon

I don't want to blame

But I feel nine months is a long time
to put up a structure that would allow us to come in
Maybe it wouldn't be as bad if a structure had been put
up
For people with dementia, anybody really
Face to face with a bit of perspex in between

All we get told is "It's in hand"
Been in hand since March
But there's nobody to blame but Covid

I would have been happy to take tests on a weekly basis
I would have funded that myself
Just to get in
But it doesn't work that way

Anon

Who's got the power?

It makes my stomach turn when I listen on the news,
still...

The clapping for the NHS workers
(I would not want to say that it's not plagued the NHS,
because of course, they're marvellous and doing a great
job)
but at that point, we were doing
the stuff that we were doing
with no recognition.
Nobody understood.
Nobody knew what was going on.
We were kind of like right on the edges,
and no support.
And this was real
And this was happening
To us.

And we are still not really acknowledged -
They're still letting people come out of hospital
with the potential of bringing it into the home.

We've only got 14 residents left
and they're bringing people back out of hospital
AGAIN
in the middle of the second wave
and we are just putting ourselves
straight back into that position

Have we learnt nothing from the last six months about
needing to protect each other?

Anon

Forgotten

There was no testing in care homes for a long time
They're as entitled as the next person,
Despite their age
It shouldn't go on your age or mentality or any other
aspect
You're a human being
You're as entitled as the next person
It's just as if –
"Oh well, they're in there, and that won't matter"
They're not to be counted, so to speak
It's as if they weren't important

Anon

Are we nearly there yet?

There isn't an end in sight
It's not as if there's a time
Usually when you have an experience of anything
you have an end to it -
A time when it ends

We still don't know what we're dealing with
The restrictions that people have in their ordinary life -
Your own recreation when you get out of work
You quite often go and get involved with something
Distracting from your normal everyday pressures
But we're very limited in what we can do

It all sounds very depressing doesn't it?

June

I don't know
I just feel so
Well not unhappy but
I just
I just -
Not very special
I don't know what to do
I don't really know
I just don't know

Anon

Slow motion

I don't like to be negative, but
Everything's going kind of slow motion.
There's nothing really to look forward to.
Everybody's feeling that little bit depressed
Everything's kind of on hold, isn't it?

Hopefully next year will be different.

Catrin

Well, I don't know how it is
It's Bad

I don't like it
That's the thing

Live round here
Have to move on

I feel
I need to move on
Yeah

Stuck in mud
That's how I feel

I don't know
About this place

I want to move on
I feel
I don't know what's wrong

Find somewhere
Enjoy
Enjoying

My place now
Miss it

I feel bad sometimes
I hope I'm alright

Used to do a lot
Wanna move on

Go where I was.
Yeah.

Miss a lot of things
From years ago
I do

Anon

We're human too

I wish families would understand it's hard for us as well
- inside

Not everybody -
but I feel families put their frustrations towards us
They forget we're in the same boat
Trying our hardest inside the homes -
to substitute the lack of interaction from the family

It's very hard and frustrating for the family
They can't come in and see their loved one
Everybody has a different opinion on it
I feel we're the front line of it -
If they're frustrated or angry
That's gonna come towards us
I wish families'd realise -
We're finding it hard too as carers

Everyone's different,
Some people are finding it harder than others
Some are more in the limelight
More likely to have the negativity put to them

Anon

Oliver Senton

Sally Anne Hughes
and Jill Longman

Jennifer Carson

Barbara Osborne

Liz
Clarke

Kunle Olaifa

June

#weareallinthistogether
Annan Court

Karen
Potter

'the family's eyes'

Family and support

Whenever we got the announcement
we were going into lockdown,
I was a 30-minute drive from my parents' house.
My parents look after my son - childcare finished at five
o'clock.

The first months of the pandemic,
I moved back home to my parents.
That was why I could be so flexible and work
because we all lived in the same house.

I would be getting a phone call at four o'clock in the
afternoon.
Can you come and do night shift?
  Yeah, that's no problem.
  Mum, you have Alex tonight I'm going into work.

Jennifer Carson

Not Just a Job

I think people should know how much the people inside
the care homes care about the residents

It's not 'just a job'

You can't say they become like part of your family,
because they are not your family but we are like family
within the home

It's not a job like any other, you know

And sometimes that's a good thing
And sometimes, that's a bad thing

Kathleen Crymble

My thoughts again

Everybody gets a floor plan
Most of my residents -
I have to do my visits with them on my own

I'm very interested in my residents
They are part of me
I'd like to do anything that will give me more
knowledge about how to support them
I'm always willing to gain more knowledge with
dementia and learn what we can do to support them

Dementia affects everybody as a subject -
What dementia is
Have you heard Bobby Charlton has been diagnosed
with dementia?
Did you know that?

Kunle Olaifa

Her wee face was so lit up

We tried to do video calls, some of our residents,
it doesn't work because
they can't see them physically,

It made me realise that
all those senses are connected.
We had one wee lady in,
her son actually brought her a pillow.
It had his aftershave on it.
We gave it to her because it was her birthday.
We wrapped it up and
I was on night shift, and she was sitting with it.
I said 'Where did you get this from?'
And she said, 'my Johnny'.
I went over and I could smell,
coz he has really distinct aftershave,
and I said, 'That is your Johnny, isn't it.'
A big smile,
'Yes.'

Jennifer Carson

It's just the situation now

She did like going out in the car, we wouldn't go very
far
because didn't really like it amongst other people and
such
but we would go and maybe go to Costa Coffee
and sit in the car, and watch people
and she would enjoy that

One of the last times I sat outside with her, in the
summer
she would be sitting there, and she'd be saying
"Roxella will be coming. She will take me out in the car
for a run"
and I'd say "I'm here, I'm here. I'm Roxella"
"Ah, alright"

It would be nice, just to do that

Roxella

Emm

I like the family
Get on well with the family
Emm
Life is like a bowl of cherries

I don't feel at the moment
Cool, calm and collected

Everything is smooth

Emm.

Anon

I feel a bit, y'know, sad for the residents
'cause they can't see their,
their family
they're always asking about them and stuff,
try to explain what's going on and,
obviously, some residents do understand
but some don't.

Seth Munday

My Extended Family

People don't know how difficult it is at times,
how hard people work to try and make their
loved ones safe as they can,
and as happy as they can be.

Also, the fact that most of us really do care.
Although they aren't our family,
they are like our family.

I don't go home and forget about them.
I go home and think,
'Okay', maybe I found something out about
somebody that day, so see what I can do to make
another day better for them.
Maybe it's just a piece of music.
Maybe it's a poem.
It doesn't matter what it is.
Just to see their smile is lovely.

Lainey

Fear

II.
Earlier in the year,
I didn't see my mother for four months,
and I'm really close to my mother.
I mean she's basically all of the family I've got, my
mother and my stepDad.
And I couldn't see them for four months,
and yet people were willy-nillying about,
and going into each other's houses,
and it was like you really don't get it.
I mean I was absolutely terrified of giving my mother
Covid.
Because I work in a hospital.
And the same now,
I haven't seen my mother in about two, two and a half
months.
You know, and -
it just gets to me when you see people who are flouting
the rules, because...
I just feel like, well, why am I doing this?
Why am I, you know, not seeing my mother,
and they're just flouting the rules and seeing everyone?

Leanne

At this moment I'm feeling good
everything is going smooth
I've got nothing to moan about
having a laugh

It's usually for a woman not
to moan about things
what my husband used to say
we did have a laugh about it

We got married, had three sons
they grow up to be good chaps

Lost my husband in the war

Like other people my mother was
a Londoner, just got to take it
on the chin, it was a family saying

Pat

My Mum

When the doors open again...
I don't think my Dad will remember me
but my Mum will

Just want to take her a gift
And hand it to her
And watch her open it
And then give her a hug

cos that was something my daughter used to say to me
when we were due to go up to the home -"Give her a
hug from me" - but she's still half a thousand miles
away...

Even if she's not fully comprehending who I am
I think there are things that click with her
After you've spoken with her for a wee while

Definitely

Irene McGinney

Children

I got a telephone so
I can spoke to my children
Think about them all the time
It's only normal for a mother to think about her children
My mother said to me –
parents are there to take care of them

Mary Obgoboh

So much love around you, if you open your eyes

I must stress, I must stress on the support that we've received -

You know, on staff, and from the personal point of view the support that I receive from the family, from my friends, from my colleagues during these difficult months...

Coming back, coming back to work as well. I feel I'm not fully recovered, health wise, but the support I received, it is so valuable.

My family lives abroad. So obviously, I couldn't go home. So those 10 minutes, quick FaceTime calls with Mum and Dad on the lunch break, gives me strength to carry on. The support I received.

Mrs Warrior113

My Mum and Dad

Lots of lovely times as well.
I contact the home and ask about my Dad.
He's only been in care for about six months
My mom looked after him - she actually sat in a chair at
the side of his bed at 89, because she didn't want him to
go in a home.
They'd been together for like, 67 years or something.
It's difficult.
But he is happy.
They Skype him every day and he's smiling.
He thinks he's in his holiday home.

He doesn't talk
But he sings.

Lainey

I think that we are families for our residents.
We are the family's hands
and we are the family's eyes,
we are the family's embrace.
We are the family's heart for these people.

I think that people have to know
in these difficult time
there are people with good hearts
caring for others.

Margarita Warburton

Sally, Sally, Pride of our alley
Sally, Sally, Pride of our alley

Don't ever wander away from the alley and me

Wendy is coming today
Yes, Wendy
Wendy, my wife

Lovely, lovely, lovely - Wendy
Always and forever
Be lovely - visiting me
Soon

Eddie

'only human'

Silver Lining

What I did is,
I was a key worker,
I got the status as a key worker
and I was looking after the disinfectant soap
and the sanitiser, mainly,
I did some shopping for the home,
papers, paperwork to the surgery,
samples to the surgery,
on my bicycle because,
in Folkestone where I live
I can get around - my bicycle - very easily.

Kitty van Geel

We are only human,
and we're allowed to be sad
and we're allowed to be scared.
Let your emotions... you're allowed to be
to feel all these things.
But don't let it bury you,
don't let it lose you.
And try to be around positive people as much
as you can. That's really it.

Sally Ann Hughes

Hello
Can we do that yet?
It will be alright, won't it?
I must get there

Will you come?
– go on

Anon

Very Lucky

As I say
I'm still enjoying it
But just as I'm getting older
I'm feeling it a little bit more!

I'm lucky
At least I've got all my limbs and I can walk
And many people can't
So, I shouldn't complain
My own Dad lost both his legs at sixty-five
That's only a year older than me now

So, I'm very lucky

Janice Dye

Ordinary Life

Sometimes ok

Somedays
Feel ok
Some days
You don't

That's it

Look at my story

That's how it is
Yeah

Have to walk on
Go your own pace

Yeah

No one else will do it
Will they

Anon

I Just Don't Know

Aye, trying to get forward with my life
Write my age on that, sixty five.

Feel fine in my own body, as healthy as I've been in my
life.

I was playing football and healthy.
Thing is, I have Alzheimer's.

The yoga I did.
The yoga I went to.
I did meditation at the beginning, it was good.
Then one day, they didn't appear.
That's one thing these people don't bother about
But if they do the yoga it's fantastic.
I used to go to work, we'd go to the hideout, we'd do it
there.

Some people would just laugh.
They just don't give it a try.

William

The Sea

Over the summer month
I could more socialise with my friends out and about.
I started swimming in the sea,
with my friends,
which gave me really a shock of freedom because,
without those regulations I felt very tied up.
I cope with nervous constructions and
I have to do it like that,
otherwise it's not a good thing,
I have to do it –

I ended once in the sea, I could let go.
I could let go, I was just enjoying my swim,
getting around and have a sense of freedom.
And it calms me down,
because I came home and realised I'd forgotten
everything.

Kitty van Geel

Look at you
YES YES AHHHHH

YES

YES YES
EI EI EI YES YES
Well, oh, oh, oh
OK

Something like that

Anon

Photos

We try and send messages or we send them photos
to sort of hopefully lift their spirits,
to think, oh gosh you know, they're,
they're sort of, you know they can still see them
in the photos, something that's poignant
like today,
I took photos of the residents,
only just colouring in a poppy, in red.
Very simple tasks,
but I took photos and they will probably be sent or
put out for the families to see
So, they can see that they're actually,
there they are,
there,
they're there in front of our eyes, you can't touch them.

Jill Longman

About life

Laying in bed

Alright actually

Not a lot

Got to do it

It's nice to know

You've done it

Anon

Cariad Mawr, Un Amor Grande

They say having two languages
is like having two souls.
Cuando tienes dos idiomas,
es como tener dos almas.

I feel the same for my two countries,
Mexico and Wales.
Because I deeply love Wales
and Mexico.
I feel I have one heart that beats for both.
Not 'between' both – 'for both'.
One is not more or less than the other.
It is the same power of love.

Margarita Warburton

Just fine
I want to pick up on it for next week
Silent
Sleeping
I feel okay.
Not that word
What did I say?
Silent.
Okay.
Yes.

Anon

The Middle

How you see yourself

I don't have anything
Happy
Nothing happy
Nothing to feel good
About myself

I used to do accounts
A job
Now I don't
Because I can't

I can't do things
Overtime
Any extra times

Anon

'The Toll of the Mask'

The Deceit

Do they know that at the very beginning
we were all working without any PPE?
I know it was in the news and things
but I think people immediately thought of hospital
and they didn't really think about care homes

I know certainly when I came home at night
I told my husband that we had PPE
so that he felt that I was safe
and I'm not a person that lies to my husband
but I reassured him that everything was okay - we had
PPE when we didn't
And also my Dad. I told my Dad that we had it

Because I didn't want them worrying about it
I didn't want them thinking 'Oh you're going into work
everyday, you could catch Covid'
'cause that's the way it would have been then, at the
beginning

You know?

Kathleen Crymble

Very tired.
All of us are very tired because we want...
we want to get it right.
If there is a right and wrong.
You want to give your best
and when you're tired
and when you've got all the buzzers going...
It can be draining at times.
But no one ever said it's easy being a carer.

Sally Ann Hughes

Very True

I have found it extremely hard to cope.
It was a tough decision for him to go into care,
but at least I could see him every other day and spend
most of the day there.
But not to see him at all,
for me, it has been absolutely devastating.

For him, I don't think he knows how long the gap has
been
Don't think he realises he's been in care now for just
over a year.
He knows about the germs,
He knows about the restrictions,
How much he remembers on a day-to-day basis, I don't
know.

Wendy

It's quite sad actually

You can see both sides, obviously:

because you work within the home
and want to protect the residents
from Covid

but you also want to protect
the residents
from the mental and emotional –
torture is the wrong word –
but they are
definitely being mentally
and emotionally affected
by the fact that they can't see
their families

Such a difficult situation for everybody
Nobody can get it right
Nobody knows what they are doing
And what to do

Kathleen Crymble

We have to look after each other

What makes up your life is the people you share it with
I can see the little, little things that they'll say,
thinking, 'I need to watch that'
'Need to keep an eye on that'

If I am worried, and I talk to them, and I say
"Is it okay, if I mentioned it to the manager?"
They say, "Oh, no, no, no, don't say anything.
I don't want them to
know I'm not doing very well. And I'm not coping"
So, I've got this constant battle all the time -
they're saying that they're not able cope
the management is saying "You've only got 18
residents, why aren't you coping?"
A massive responsibility and pressure on me
Thinking 'Oh, my God, we should be coping'
No - they're going through the pandemic
we're all in it
together

Piling on extra pressure when they say they
aren't coping, going to send them into a tailspin

Anon

Go Away Covid

Fffft...
Oh dear God.
Awful* Oh*
No' Bad, No' Bad, No' Bad, No' Bad
Hellish....
Hellish...
No' a bad day.
That's nothing new is it.
*

Get me out of here.
Fffft.

You laughed here

Anon

The Toll of The Mask

The word depressing is often taken out of context,
and used far too frequently.
However,
if you look at the actual definition of the word,
you know, it's a very suppressed time, everybody's
unable to see their family and their friends,
they're unable to mix socially -
and we're essentially -
human beings are social creatures.
You can't see somebody smile behind a mask,
you can only see their eyes,
and although the eyes are the window of
the soul, you still can't see their lips,
you can't see the expression,
you can't touch people in the way you would
previously.

So, I think overall
that, across a prolonged period of weeks, and now
months,
is having a toll on the people that have really stuck by
the rules and behaved themselves.

Jacqui Offen

Just Show Love

It's hard to open up sometimes.
I think when you care for somebody, you don't always
care about yourself.
You need to take that time, I'm realising.

Coz if I'm strong, I can be strong for them.
I'm a softy anyway
I cry at Bambi when film comes on so...
It's better out than in
I always tell them that when they're crying.

Karen Potter

Touch

I'm struggling a lot because of Mum
Since Covid it's 10 times - 100 times worse
I've had to go on to some antidepressants
They are helping but then I lost a close friend
We had his funeral this week
It's just like everything seems to come at once

Even at a funeral you can't have that contact
It's the contact I'm struggling with
That I can't get close to people
Even my kids when they come -
I can't hug them or whatever
It's very, very hard
And it does have a knock-on effect

Lynne Ellis

Put them down

Doing this
I'm doing this

So they can see

There's more than one thing
You can work on

Don't always improve
Gives work on
Not sensible
But

Put them down
Words

Like to think
Help people
Feel good about themselves
On the opposite

What I knew
I think that's what I knew

Just bits
Something to make
Into
Something

Anon

I don't think he'll live longer than two years, the way
he's deteriorated

You just don't know which way to turn for the best.
Well, I certainly don't.
I don't really think I need medications for anxiety and
depression,
I've coped so far,
I don't want tablets to help me through it.
I think I'm stronger than that.

But who knows what'll happen in two or three years
time?
Somehow, I don't think David will be here
in two or three years.
They usually say the life of somebody that goes into
care home with dementia is 18 months or two years.
And I can believe that.

Mavis Eyre

You lose some

It's not a nice time to be in the caring profession
It's not nice
We've lost girls - they've just said they can't - can't cope
with the loss all the time and the pressure and the
responsibility
Just not what they want

People don't want to admit that they're not dealing with
it
Don't admit when not coping
And if you are not strong enough, what happens to you?
We are not all mentally the same
Not strong in the same ways
People with mental health problems are far stronger in
a lot of ways
Strength comes in lots of different packages
But we find it hard to admit we can't or don't want to do
it
Choice. Some people don't have choices.

Anon

Mental Health

Do you know what?

I've been suffering with anxiety a bit recently
I think any normal person my age has been
who's been working with care
Struggled with it

Come out the other end
Starting to feel a bit stronger now

When we were all on lock down I did suffer a lot:
I couldn't see my loved ones,
I couldn't see friends
You're on your own and you've got to work
Got no one around you apart from your work colleagues

Chloe

The old me

It's definitely brought out some of the best
and some of the worst in me.
Completely split me.
Because
I feel passionate - more passionate - about the
residents
Before lockdown I was caring, of course, I
wanted the best
Wanted to make sure they had quality of life.
I think I feel more passionate for them.
So that's amazing, that's brilliant.
But the flip side, the knock-on effect is
I've lost the passion for any other kind of life
the old get up and go and the want, the drive
all the other things I used to do
All the things that used to keep you sane
keep you happy on your days off
Build your strength back up to go back into work again
We've had all of those taken away from us

Liz Clarke

Don't Know

Difficult
Strange.
Unknown.
I don't know. I guess what we've all got used to.
Because everyday is -
Every day is
Difficult And Strange.

Suzanne Elliot

BETTER

It could be better
I'm not going to start
Outline the problem
We have lived through worst
Don't like being a women
I think men have a lot of advantages

Mary Obgoboh

The All Singing, All Dancing Show

Summat can happen in the days and
they'll give you a smile,
and it's all worth it.
Whatever's happenin' out there can stay outside –
in here it's completely different.

We wear a mask – two masks –
one when we're scared, and the other one
we don't show any scaredness,
'coz we've got to be strong.
And that's what's we're doing.
Sometimes it's hard.

Karen Potter

A better side

What is life?
Sometimes ok
But
Get mixed up
Way down
Somewhere
All gone
Work it out somehow
Work it out
Find a way
Have to
Work it out

Somehow
Bit of a story
Lots of things I wanna change
But I got here
Crazy

Anon

I care because I love to

It is tough
Someone's got to do it

I love it
Making a difference to people's lives
I'd never go back to work where there's not really a
point

When you care, you love

It's an important part of someone's life –
To make the decision to go into a care home
Being part of someone's life at the end
It's Amazing

I've my own personal mental health battles
Living with depression and caring for others
helps make me feel like my life is worth living
Because someone relies on me
I'm helping someone else –
Making a difference to someone's life rather than just
making someone else richer

It's a special job and only certain people can do it

Abi Watt

I just wanna be getting back
Y'know

Cos there's a lot of people
About here

There is here
But not outside

There's something very nice
in that book

That's come out
Then next minute it's all gone

I just want to get back
Just had enough of it really

Well, I'm feeling alright
Doing alright

Anon

184

Fine

Everyone is fine and having a good time
I cannot concentrate
Close the door.

Righteousness and forgiveness.

Edna

When you get good care, my goodness, they are worth a million.

They should be looked after better.

They're going home,
coming straight back to work, going home, and
straight back to work.
Because they don't want to bring back Covid into
their work.

Because it only takes one person to bring it in
Staff have been so good.

And when you speak to them, they're so
upbeat and happy.
I've never ever had a phone call from
any of the girls – and they speak to you
all the time, and the manager – of being
downtrodden or anything.
They're always upbeat.

Always willing to talk to you and they'll tell you if
something's wrong.

Barbara Osborne

Motivation

We cherish
we value people around us
and we open our eyes and recognise
elderly people, vulnerable people
even more now.

I work in a care home for a reason
It was my choice. I'm a qualified teacher
but I didn't want to pursue that

I'd like to believe that it does make a difference -
Today, tomorrow, in the future,
even if on the moment, I can bring a smile
and maybe by tomorrow it will be forgotten
but that feeling...

That's something they never forget.
I like to believe that.

Mrs Warrior113

It is so, so difficult, you know
Unless you are in that predicament
then I don't think you have any sense whatsoever
how hard it must be on the carers
they'll miss the company too
they've all got their families
they've got the worry
And they're trying to keep everything going

I know that the one girl last week
gave up her day off to go in and do some lady's hair
you can't replace kindness like that
really thoughtful
I know that when I get my hair done, I feel better
Just the simple things

And some people heard and said "Why haven't you
done my Mother?"
It's a no-win situation really

                                                    Roxella

Red Tape

They probably don't realise the number
of policies that we get
- guidelines and policies - relating to Covid-19

they change weekly, dependent on what's happening

We have policies every week that we have to make
sure
we know and understand
every nurses' station got one
for carers to read - one in the staff room

You know, I think there is an awful lot that the relatives
don't get and maybe they do take for granted
we've obviously got to follow guidelines and policies
before we can even think about letting relatives back in
here
there is so much red tape that we have to abide by
for the sake of us, the relatives and the residents

Suzanne Elliot

Safety

With the whole thing of the numbers risin',
you're going into work each week and
Have we got cases, have we not got cases?

The early days, it was very fearful times.
When we started routinely testing staff and residents
that was another minefield,
trying to explain to the residents
why they had to get this cotton bud put down their
throat and up their nose every x amount of weeks.

Some, of course, refused.

We had to try again with them.

Jennifer Carson

Element of luck

We got through the whole of the last lockdown
Bearing in mind that we didn't have face masks on
And travelling in
It's an element of luck
because sometimes you don't know you're carrying it
And it doesn't matter how much hand washing you do
If you're carrying it and you're close to somebody
That's why we're wearing masks now

So, you can only do your best to kind of minimise the
risk.
Doesn't matter how much testing we do
Because if you've got, it spreads

And the nature of the work,
when you're washing somebody
the two-metre rule can't apply

Marian Howell

We are working hard

Residents and family,
they are suffering, and isolated.
I'd like people to take it seriously
and not blame the care homes,
not blame the carers, with cases in the homes.

Our care home, we've worked so hard,
we've worked extra shifts to keep agency workers out,
coz they go from home to home – to make it safer.
We've missed days with our partners and stuff,
doing days and nights.

                                                    Catrin

Making A Difference

It is quite difficult
because you're giving so much of yourself to someone –
well to a multitude actually.
But it's worth it.

You know when you get a little smile, or they touch
your hand.
I've had someone kiss my visor, which they're not
supposed to do!
But...

How can you stop them?
You know, they do it before you even realise what
they're doing.
And it makes you realise you've made a small difference
if nothing else.

I think in these times it's difficult to make a large
difference.

Leanne

We are in here
And we've been in here
And we're going to continue being in here

We are in our own little world as such
Because we have to be so careful with who is
allowed in the buildings
And we have had to just be everything
We've had to be friends, sisters,
mothers, fathers,
And it's all in the name of keeping them
alive
We have to do everything we can to
keep them safe as a duty of care

Anon

You Do Get Fed Up With Things

I'm getting a bit fed up with having to wear these
masks.
And washing your hands thoroughly every day,
when you get in and when you get out.
And it's a bit depressing when they talk about the
deaths,
so many deaths, so many people infected.
There's not a good track and trace system yet,
and they say they'll probably get a remedy, an
inoculation in the next month or so.
So, let's hope,
let's hope that's true.
I don't know maybe I've read the wrong paper

Jenny

Do you know what I love doing?
When I was visiting my Dad, when I go around,
I sit down, have a cup of tea and a chat with my Dad,
We'd always have the telly on as the wallpaper
Anyways, to cut a long story short,
I got hooked on Tipping Point
And my way to relax (my husband and my daughter,
they mock me and tease me!)
What I love doing is - when I get to my Dad's,
I say, "Dad, quick, quick! Turn it over to ITV, ITV 1"
He'll have his Rum
I keep yelling the questions
"What's that Dad? What's that?"
To get him to answer the questions
And we watch the Tipping Point
I find it very relaxing,
Watching the machine pushing the coins back and
forth,
and tipping them over the edge

When I'm not visiting my Dad,
I come home
Make sure I have a proper stretch after cycling
Then I sit cross legged on the sofa
Get myself a cafe latte
And then I watch Tipping Point
That's how I switch off

Samantha Jones

We plod on because we love it.
We plod on because...
we definitely don't do it for the money,
I can tell you.

It is a passion, isn't it?
I think it's a passion to care for people.

One day, I hope they'll pay us a lot of money.
I don't think it'll be anytime soon.
But for the time being, I come back and I feel...
I feel I've been of use.

That's the main thing, I've given something.
And hopefully it's been in a positive way.

Sally Ann Hughes

Shazea Quraishi

Zoë Aldrich

Kay

Jacqui Offen

198

Seth Munday

Megan Whitworth

Barbara

Susan McCallum

Ceri Clark

'Raise your voices!'

Every resident we have here is somebody's family
Somebody's loved one
Or they were in the past
They haven't got anybody now
But they are our grandparents
They are best friends
They are sisters
They are brothers
They are Mums
They are Dads
And they deserve the absolute best possible quality of
care, the quality of life, that they can have

And they don't get it
Because of the system, because of the way it works

We do the absolute best we can for them
But I think the whole system-
There's such a gaping hole in what it should be,
compared to what we've got

Anon

Voices

"We've only got a few residents now, we
don't need all the staff"

Well I say, we do need the staff because
residents can now have a better quality of
life
be more people to give them that quality
instead of everybody just running around
like headless chickens trying to get
everything done
they're not on the floor
they're focussing too much about what can
we prove at the next
inspection

We've been doing everything that we can
That's why what you are doing
and what we are part of is important
Because people aren't going to be listened to
Aren't going to be listened to at all

Because of Covid many have lost
their voice altogether
When they were talking, nobody was listening
Some of our residents have just stopped
talking People are whizzing past them,
being busy, doing tasks
It's important to sit down and hold their
hand, and talk to them.

Anon

The Best Life

The whole world needs to be talking about dementia,
Needs to understand that life doesn't end just because
you get dementia.

The lives of people with dementia can be just as
fulfilling
yes, they can't do everything that they would
have been able to do before their diagnosis,
But they can still do a lot of things that will make them
feel good -
And that's what life is really about
Finding what makes you feel good
And you keep doing it

There's no reason why, when you get dementia, that
that should change
It might be harder to work out what makes you feel
good,
It might change on a daily basis,
And you might have to start again the next day to figure
out what's going to make you feel good,
But every day you should strive to find something that
makes you feel good

Naomi Daglish

It's structural:

i)
The spotlight's been shined upon the whole care system
There's a lot of talk - but
Until you actually treat caring as a profession
Not on the miniMum wage
Nothing will change

It needs a lot of diverse talents to be a good carer
Treat it as a profession
Treat it with respect

ii)
I don't think it's the carers' fault
It's all needing a massive funding increase

A lot of people are very committed and trying very hard
But it's at breaking point
It needs a massive overhaul of the system

Stephen Bill

The Four Nations

I was just thinking...

At the end of this, we should be petitioning all the care home owners to pay double the wages of the carers.

I wonder if part of it is because... I almost felt at the beginning that the elderly were dispensable.

I think it's improved and after it's all over there'll be some kind of public enquiry and they'll be ashamed of themselves. When I say 'they' I mean all governments, of the four nations.

But then, you know, you sympathise that they were dealing with a hundred and one million things brought up by Covid.

We are just a wee after thought.

Anon

Raise your voices!!

I think there are a lot of people out there that would
like to shout
Louder
but they don't

Residents families are dealing with
Everything about it
All encompassing
Overwhelming

I would like to shout from the rooftops
"Care homes shouldn't be forgotten"
They have been
It's time somebody did something about it

Irene McGinney

Thanks to the carers

I couldn't do that job.
I couldn't be a carer like they do.
I think they're wonderful, wonderful people.
They deserve what's best in life, in my opinion
And they don't get it.

What they give them as wages - they ought to have a lot
more.
They're the kind of people who're really, really good.

I'm afraid I just couldn't do it
It'd break my heart.

Mavis Eyre

Sod the consequences

Word gets trickled down from on high
"When this is all over, we'll have some sort of
ceremony, a remembrance ceremony for the
people that we've lost".
Which is absolutely wonderful.

But what we need to come down at the
moment is "You're all doing a fantastic job, and
we really appreciate everything that you're
doing"

Maybe I just need to be a little bit more telling
and sod the consequences.

Anon

'Living, living'

The Light at the End of the Tunnel

Well, here with the patients
patients don't know what's going on, apart from the,
y'know,
exceptional one or two, or three.
So, I just want our patients to know that they're safe.
They're safe here.
And, I want people to know there will be a silver lining.
Things will improve.

Jenny

Look at all that writing
Thank you so much
I can't lay it down to do it
No, can't

Anon

You see. Happy.
Yes, I will, love with you. Look at that.

Ooo... you are the <u>best</u> of the week.
Can you do on those?
Och, its lovely, at the moment.

Anon

Definitely

Life is still going on around us.
Things are still happening apart from
Covid. People are in difficult positions,
hurricanes in different countries...
And I think it just puts added pressure on people.

But life is for living
You've just got to make the best you can
out of the situation at the moment.
Even if it's just dancing in the kitchen with
the music on
Which I've been known to do.

Lainey

I gotta gotta

And two and two

In to do

Comma comma

                                        Al

I Am Quite Happy

As happy as a pig in poo.
Oh ya.
Come again.
I can't think of anything better, it's a happy life.
Oh, it is.
Beautiful.
Can't complain.
Hmm, hmm.
Ya.
Any more questions?
Beautiful.
Great.
Oh ye.

Hollis Jones

Angela's girl

I'm feeling absolutely wonderful. I was going in to get a
new one. Some very kind person gave me theirs. I'm
feeling just a little bit down but nothing like here.
Everything for me has got so much better. The people
that come are very nice. If they want something they
should go and get it. All in all I'm a very lucky girl. Yes.

Anon

As I'm speaking to you now
I'm looking out the window, and,
Touch wood,
We've got a beautiful view where we live, we're in
North Islington, in an old house on the top of a hill

I've got a skyline of London
I'm just looking at the sea of trees
The city skyline
The sun going down
And it's beautiful

I'm so grateful for that
So bloody grateful for that
So it's just made me appreciate things even more,
not that I didn't appreciate them before,
but even *more* so

And also to pinch myself and slap myself
when I'm moaning and groaning about petty things -
Not to get not to get me knickers in a twist
as much as I used to,
Not to get me knickers in a twist!

Samantha Jones

To be loved
and to give love -
Some people aren't,
and can't give it either

That is why I keep saying I'm lucky

We can always be miserable and unkind and horrible
But there's no need to be like that

If you've got people around you that know you, and care
for you,
It gives you a better outlook on life
I'm just sad some people haven't

Love and be loved

Anon

7.

I think with all the experiences that I kind of gained,
from the
home
I've got a completely different outlook on life now and,
seeing the things that people went through and,
going through that myself, just made me have
a more positive outlook,
and be very grateful for, life, I suppose.

Megan Whitworth

Living
Living
I want to live live live
That's it, what else I can put
Live
Live
That's it
Can't think of anything else, can you?

Elsie

Nature reflection

I have always managed to find something
Nature is always there

I go out to watch the sunrise
Watch the birds
Their names, where they came from, the family
Watch swans, geese

Today for instance
I noticed two new ones
I got pictures
Two geese with five babies
So I collect pictures
I watch them

It's not ending
Life doesn't end when you have such things
Always something there to focus on

Kunle Olaifa

INDEX

Please excuse our crude indexing here.

PD   Project participant living with a dementia
RL   Relative project participant
CS   Care or nursing home staff project participant
RS   Resident project participant, without a dementia

THE KEY
Well, I feel   PD
Helpless   RL
The Most Difficult Thing   RL
'Because, because'   RL
Frustration   RL
So Sad   RL
The Key   PD
Love is the only word really   RL
Emotional to see her   RL
Heart wrenching   RL
'I am frustrated at the moment'   PD
Here   CS
Losing Nanna   RL
Hold my hand   RL
Change 2   CS
Why me?   RL
Frustrations and perseverance   RL
Acceptance   RL
I will remember that   RL
Joy   RL
'I feel okay today'   PD
Pain of relationships   CS
Another world   RL
Deeply Sad   RL
Unfair   RL

UNTETHERED
Floating Around   PD
Segregation   RL
11.   RL
Lost   RL
Sad times   RL
Two observations   PD
Lost time   CS

Forgotten people	RL
Loneliness	CS
Just living	CS
'I think, I feel and I see this double isolation'	CS
Canadian Pacific	PD
'Without you I'm wasted'	PD
The need for human contact	RL
Support	CS
'Very good'	PD

HE'S STILL THERE
'Shock'	RL
12.	CS
So much has changed	CS
Losing touch	RL
It's just a blur again	CS
The hard times	CS
Losing Friends	RL
'It's like a bereavement but she's still here'	RL
Guilt	RL
It's best to talk about it	RL
I'm grieving	RL
'Awful'	PD
'But of course, there's a great deal of guilt'	RL

PART OF THE PICTURES
Rooms	CS
1.	CS
4.	CS
Family	CS
It is how I feel	RL
'Shutdown happened on the 23rd of March'	RL
Making Light of a Bad Situation	CS
We learned how to work in a team	CS
Muffled Words	CS
90	PD
In through the nose, out through the mouth	RL
TV	PD
'You have to live in hope'	RL
A smile wins it all	CS
Part of the pictures	PD
Digital – the answer?	CS
Close Contact	CS
6.	CS

226

STAY ON THE SAME LINE
We Are Fighting You, COVID   CS
'One of the carers I spoke to'   RL
Solidarity   CS
'If they can live through a war...'   CS
Cariad Mawr, Un Amor Grande 2   CS
My Personal Rollercoaster   CS
Don't Forget   CS

ARE WE NEARLY THERE YET?
She wouldn't be able to answer me now   RL
The Abandonment   CS
Sums it up   PD
Don't like being critical   CS
Written down   PD
Who Cares?   RL
Boredom Area   PD
I don't want to blame   RL
Who's got the power?   CS
Forgotten   RL
Are we nearly there yet?   CS
'I don't know'   PD
Slow motion   CS
'Well, I don't know how it is'   PD
We're human too   CS

THE FAMILY'S EYES
Family and support   CS
Not just a Job   CS
My thoughts again   CS
Her wee face was so lit up   CS
It's just the situation now   RL
Emm   PD
'I feel a bit, y'know, sad for the residents'   CS
My Extended Family   CS
Fear   CS
'At this moment I'm feeling good'   PD
My Mum   RL
Children   PD
So much love around you, if you open your eyes   CS
My Mum and Dad   CS
'I think that we are families for our residents'   CS
'Sally, Sally, Pride of our alley'   PD

227

ONLY HUMAN
Silver Lining CS
'We are only human' CS
'Hello' PD
Very Lucky CS
Ordinary Life PD
I Just Don't Know PD
The Sea CS
'Look at you' PD
Photos CS
'About life' PD
Cariad Mawr, Un Amor Grande CS
'Just fine' PD
The Middle PD

THE TOLL OF THE MASK
The Deceit CS
'Very tired' CS
Very true RL
It's quite sad actually CS
We have to look after each other CS
Go away Covid PD
The Toll of The Mask RL
Just Show Love CS
Touch RL
Put them down PD
'I don't think he'll live longer than...' RL
You lose some CS
Mental Health CS
The old me CS
Don't Know CS
BETTER PD
The All Singing, All Dancing Show CS
A better side PD
I care because I love to CS
'I just wanna be getting back' PD
Fine PD
When you get good care... RL
Motivation CS
'It is so, so difficult, you know' RL
Red Tape CS
Safety CS
Element of luck CS
228

We are working hard	CS
Making A Difference	CS
'We are in here'	CS
You Do Get Fed Up With Things	CS
'Do you know what I love doing?'	RL
'We plod on because we love it'	CS

RAISE YOUR VOICES!

'Every resident we have here ...'	CS
Voices	CS
The Best Life	CS
It's structural	RL
The Four Nations	CS
Raise your voices!!	RL
Thanks to the carers	RL
Sod the consequences	CS

LIVING, LIVING

The Light at the End of the Tunnel	CS
'Look at all that writing'	PD
'You see. Happy'	PD
Definitely	CS
'I gotta gotta'	PD
I Am Quite Happy	PD
Angela's girl	PD
'As I'm speaking to you now'	RL
'To be loved'	RS
7.	CS
Living	PD
Nature reflection	CR

Thanks

We would like to thank everyone who has made this project and book possible, including the following individuals and organisations:

Special thanks to Sandra Seaton who was instrumental in the idea behind this book but was sadly, unable to take part; Susan Allen; Bill Nash; Christopher Hartley; Natalie Smith; Kate Howard; Sam Carlisle; Ewan Golder; Krish Majumdar; Olivia Franklin; Rachel Walker; Danuta Lipinska; Sarah Penney; Hilary Woodhead; Steph Thompson; Cathrina Moore; George Dewis; Andy Aitchison; Laurence Pears; For collating and editing Shazea Quraishi and Susanna Howard; Trustees Sasha Bruce and Reinhard Guss; Kent Libraries; Creative Folkestone; All at Glassworks, Folkestone; NAPA; My Home Life; National Care Forum; Arts Council England; Kent Community Foundation; National Lottery Community Fund; FHCLCT.

Enormous hugs of solidarity and strength to everyone named and unnamed whose words form this book, and to your friends, families and the loved ones around you.

Further thanks to the generosity of Brian Cox, and the Cox family; Vic Rayner; Professor Sebastian Crutch; Christopher Eccleston; Alison Steadman; Meera Syal; Jane Moore; Bidisha; Keith Oliver; and Nula Suchet for supporting our work with your words.

Heartfelt thanks of support to the care homes and groups working on this project, they included: Advinia Health Care; Annan Court residential care home; Woodstock residential care home; West Ridings residential and nursing care home; The Red House care home; 73 Mildmay; Notting Hill Genesis Group; Butterworth Centre care home; Sanctuary Care; The Chapel House nursing home; Plessington Court care home; Kingsgate nursing home; Cwmbran House care home; Wood Green care and nursing home, Newtonabbey; Madeira Lodge care home; Belmont Healthcare; Tudor Lodge care home; Sai care homes; St Margaret's nursing home; Simicare Ltd. All power to you.

And finally, thanks to the three amazing action learning teams who took part in what was, after all, a pilot project to see if Living Words could translate and work remotely. You made this happen. Keep going. And see you on the Living Words tour bus! You are the: Superfluous Covid Superstars; Yellow No No Bee Gees; and the Three o'clock Amigo Aves. This is for you.

Feedback for 'Bringing the Inside Out', project 2020

'These sessions have really impacted on this lady - she talks much more, she is much brighter, and her daughter noticed this' *K*

'I was sceptical at first but now, at the end of the project, I am amazed' *L*

'I am surprised what's come, when I sit down and try to do this. One lady, who is at very late stage, I don't think there is long - I was surprised at what she came out with, it has all been very, very interesting' *L*

'It's been lovely doing this project, meeting you all, all your passion. It's been lovely to sit and ponder at our residents' words. When you see them in black and white you can see what they really mean' *J*

'From a glimmer of an idea, you've changed all these people's lives.... we haven't been able to touch or hug, things are missing and in a way this project has given me, my carers and relatives - not even mentioning the people with dementia here - a kind of virtual hug, you've given it back. It feels to me like a healing, I'm healing' *Liz*

'They're invaluable on many levels and will be a record/legacy of each of the individuals who live there' *Samantha, Daughter of Resident*

'It has been a very worthwhile experience and already has helped me in my everyday work and I am so glad I was asked to take part in the project. I would like to say a big thank you to everyone I met through the Living Words project' *Anon*

'I have discussed with X's wife and she was absolutely so pleased reading his words, she said reading them she felt 'connected' to him as she – in a way – recognised his words' *S*

Leaving a Legacy Gift or Making a Donation

Leaving a gift or donation to a charity that you view as valuable to your individual beliefs, as well as to society, ensures a legacy, as the charity continues to transform the lives of individuals and communities, into the future.

Living Words Arts is a charity that survives on funding and thoughtful contributions. Our projects make a difference to those experiencing a dementia, particularly advanced dementia, and for those who care for them. We also run projects with people experiencing mental ill health and isolation. Gifts help us continue our vision of enabling our life-enhancing work to reach more people.

A legacy gift need not be a part of the final chapter in a person's life story, more a beginning of something new. 'In Memory' donations can also be a comfort to friends and family, and a practical reminder of a loved one. Any gift left in your will is confidential and will be treated with respect.

"It's now more than two years since Dad gave Susanna his words and laughed with her, and spoke some actually quite profound words. They show his intellect and his consideration, of all sorts of things. This project has meant a massive amount to me, because I have those words, I have that book, I have the composition that Living Words created - 'It's a Funny Old World' - the song that is Dad's words. It's a legacy which I have that I can play and enjoy and read and remember. Even with late-stage dementia, my father remained, and remains today, the same intelligent man who still has a smile in his eyes. Living Words have been instrumental in giving me a lot of joy through that." *Jacqui Offen*

How can I give a Gift or make a Donation?

Click the donate button on our website www.livingwords.org.uk or get in touch to start a conversation: info@livingwords.org.uk / 07967 502 506